How to Write a CV

if you have
little or no
work experience

A Guide for Students
and Recent Graduates

ISBN 978-0-9929202-6-5

How to Write a CV
if you have
little or no
work experience

A Guide for Students
and Recent Graduates

Vlad Mackevic

HALLOW BOOKS

Contents

No experience? No problem!

Hello, and thank you for picking up my book!

So, you've found a job advertisement. Maybe it's a student job, maybe an internship or perhaps you're a recent graduate looking for some serious work but you are not quite sure how to show your prospective employer that you're brilliant. Perhaps over the course of your studies you've heard some contradictory opinions. Some people say that your grades do not matter that much – your experience does – so if you have a first-class degree, someone else with a 2:1 (or even 2:2) and more work experience than you will be chosen over you. Other people say that your grades do matter and a person with better grades will be chosen if both candidates have similar work experience.

In fact, both opinions are right. They just apply to different situations. If you are applying for an internship at the end of your first year of university, your academic performance is often the main indicator of how hard-working and serious you are. For a graduate job, work experience is more important, but grades can also play a role. But what if you are like the majority of students? What if you've only worked as a waiter during your university years and belonged to a few student groups and societies? That does not sound too impressive. How can you show a potential employer that you're brilliant?

In this book, I will try to answer these questions.

Both students and recent graduates are faced with the same problem: how to write a good CV/Résumé when you have little or no work experience; how to be taken seriously when so little of that experience is relevant to the job you are applying for. There are no absolute rules, but this book will provide you with a lot of tips to stimulate your creativity.

This book aims to answer several very important questions:

- What skills are almost all employers looking for?
- How do you present yourself professionally?
- How can you extract valuable information from the little work experience you've got?
- How do you present your work experience so that it looks impressive?
- What should you do if you've never had a paid job?
- How important are the duties and responsibilities at the workplace?
- What is more important – the duties or the achievements?
- How do you write covering letters and application forms that will get you interviews?

What is more, this book gives you advice on how to get work experience and what counts as work experience.

This book is a great resource for students and recent graduates who are just starting their careers. I also acknowledge that people's situations are different and that the job-search needs of a first year student might be different from those of a graduate. For this reason, I will try to cover as many situations as possible in these pages. Enjoy reading!

Chapter 1

Two Basic Types of CVs
and Why You Need One in the First Place

A CV does not get you a job. That is not why people write CVs. Instead, it gets you *an interview*. The purpose of the CV is to make your employer interested in you enough for them to want to meet you in person. Therefore, a CV is all about *presenting yourself*. The main task, when writing a CV, is to make every single small achievement of yours look like a big thing. I will come back to this later in this chapter and in this book.

There are two main types of CVs – those based on experience and those based on skills. Naturally, the first type is more popular. It is the usual type of CV that gives a lot of space to describing work experience. So how do you compete in a job market if you have little or no 'serious' work experience?

Well, the answer is simple: you focus your CV on your skills and achievements. You focus not on what your tasks and responsibilities were but what you *learnt* during the limited experience that you have.

I am absolutely certain that, even if your work experience as a student hardly extends beyond the traditional range of jobs (cashier, bartender, waiter/waitress, salesperson, etc.), you can still present yourself as a well-rounded individual with a set of skills that will make you as competitive as a working professional. Moreover, this book explains how to use the fact that you're a student to your advantage. There are many ways to gain valuable and serious work experience. The tips are scattered across the book and you can also find them in **Chapter 15.**[1]

Let me tell you one thing from the start: even in a job that is 'un-cool' or unpaid, or both, the most important thing is not *what* you did, but *how* you did it. What did you achieve? What skills did you develop? How can you apply those skills at the new workplace? This is what you have to think about. This book provides you with examples of those skills and teaches you how to present them.

> *Remember this:*
> *Many people know how to cook but*
> *only great cooks also know how to*
> *serve the food!*

---

[1] By the way, I have also written another book that focuses on how to make yourself more employable while you are a student. The book is called *Fight for that Job! How to become employable while you are still at university.* The book is available to buy online, from Amazon.

A CV is all about self-presentation. It has to be clear, concise and full of powerful words. It is all about presenting your every little achievement as if it were the biggest thing in the world! And you are not lying or exaggerating here – it *is* the biggest thing. For *you*. In *your* life.

So let's see how to do it!

Any Writing Is a Craft: And It Can Be Learnt!

Writing is hard work – just ask any writer about that and they will confirm it. Writing a CV is also hard work. That is why I wrote this book: to make your job easier. Because CV writing (or, in fact, any writing) does not simply come from inspiration. No book, no article, no two-page document was ever written just because great ideas beamed from the sky into the writer's head. It is a craft and it can be learnt if you know the techniques.

On the following pages, I will provide two made-up examples of CVs. One is experience-based and the other one is skills-based. I will analyse both of them, and make a list of elements of which a CV is made. Later in this book, I will write more about each of these elements, especially focussing on how to present your work experience and skills. The majority of the focus of this book will be on skills-based CVs, but the advice I give also applies to experience-based CVs and you can use it later during your career.

Ms Jane Smith[1]

Flat 1, 16 Anywhere Road, Anytown, AN1 5AB[2]

E-mail Jane.Danielle.Smith@gmail.com[3] **Tel. 07123 456 789[4]**

Education[5]

Anycity University   **2010 – 2014[6]**
BSc Marketing and Management, 2:1

Anytown Sixth Form College   **2008 – 2010**
A-levels: Mathematics (B); Business Studies (A); Spanish (B); Media Studies (A)

Work Experience[7]

Events and Contracts Manager   **Feb 2016 – Present**
Dandelion Hotel, Anytown

- Responsible for organising over 70 events annually, leading a team of 8 staff members;
- Responsible for marketing activities and presentations during events; increased the customer base by 15% since the start of 2017.[8]
- Amplified my leadership, team work, planning and organisational skills.[9]

Marketing Executive
ABC Media, Anycity
Aug 2014 – Jan 2016

- Organised and delivered marketing presentations at over 120 events across the city; attracted eight high-profile clients (multinationals and government bodies) and over 90 clients in total;[10]
- Actively liaised with stakeholders and prospective clients; enhanced my communication, negotiation and public speaking skills;[11]
- Actively learnt on the job; gained valuable knowledge about the market side of media services;

Marketing and Events Assistant
Anycity University (work placement)
Jul 2012 – Aug 2013

- Took an active role in the organisation of events around the academic year, especially the graduation and the Welcome Fortnight for new students;
- Managed the Fresher Buddy scheme (second year students mentoring first years), involving 30[12] volunteer mentors;
- Received positive feedback from my supervisor on my pro-active approach and excellent organisational skills.

IT Skills[13]

- Proficient user of MS Office Applications (Advanced User certificates for PowerPoint and Excel);
- Experience in blogging and internet publishing; familiar with most major blogging platforms;

The example CV on pages 6 and 7 of this book is experience-based. As you can see, this type of CV is only one page long (skills-based CVs can be two pages long) and the main focus is this person's work experience. I must say, however, that if you have more experience, it is perfectly fine to write an experience-based CV that is two pages long.

The experience-based CV is usually written by people with a significant amount of work experience in one field (in this case it is marketing). Jane Smith is probably looking for a new job in the field of marketing, given her experience. On the other hand, skills-based CVs are written by people who either (a) do not have a lot of experience at all; (b) have had a number of different jobs in a range of fields or (c) simply want a career change after working in a certain field for some time.

Let us analyse Jane's CV in detail. As I mentioned before, a lot of what I say about experience-based CVs applies to skills-based ones as well. I will go through the elements of Jane's CV one by one, commenting on them

1. The name. The only thing that should appear in the first line of your CV is your name. Do not write the words *Curriculum Vitae, CV* or *Résumé* at the top of the document. Your employer knows that they are reading a CV and not a crime novel. Your name looks much better and more professional.

2. Your address. This is rather straightforward: your contact details should be right at the top. Besides your address, you should also include your email address (3) and phone number (4). If you are writing a two-page CV, then

type your name and phone number into the footer. This way, the employer will be able to contact you even if the first page is lost.

3. Email address. Your email address should look professional. The best option is the following format: *name.surname@website.com* or *name_surname@website.com*. Do not put 'funny' email addresses like *kill_the_clown@yahoo.com* or *kitty.blue.eyes_xoxo@gmail.com.* These look very unprofessional.

4. Phone number. Make sure that your phone number is current and if you happen to lose the number, update your CV immediately: write the new number and print several copies.

5. Education. It is important to list your education in reverse chronological order – that is, the most recent education should be mentioned first. I will write more about the Education section of your CV in **Chapter 5: Education.**

6. You do not need to mention the month when you started or finished college or university. Everyone knows that the academic year starts in September/October and ends in June/July, so just write the years.

7. Work experience. Just like in the education section, the most recent job should be listed first. I will talk more about the Work Experience section later in this book, in **Chapter 7: Work Experience and the Lack of It.**

8; 10; 12. When writing about your work experience, it is important to emphasise your achievements. It is also important that these achievements are measureable: ideally, they should include some numbers, but there are many ways achievements can be measured. I will talk about this later in this book as well.

9; 11. Another thing you can mention when describing your work experience is which skills you developed in that job.

13. It is a good idea to add a Skills section in your experience-based CV. However, that section should not contain information about your 'soft skills' like communication, teamwork or time management. Rather, you should include 'hard skills', such as languages, if you speak any, and IT and computing skills. I will write more about it in **Chapter 8: Presenting your Skills.**

There are also a number of things you should not include in your CV – they are unnecessary and it is even unacceptable for the employers to ask for some of this information. These are:

(a) Your nationality. This information is mostly irrelevant. Companies have different policies regarding recruitment (for example, in order to get a job in the field of national security you should be a national of the country). However, many multinational companies hire people from all over the world and the only thing that matters are their skills. Under the current European law, British companies can choose to hire a person from any country that is a member of the European Economic Area and they should not discriminate based on nationality.

(b) Your marital status. It is nobody's business if you are married, are about to get married, are pregnant, are planning to have children or already have them. Your employer should not discriminate against you based on any of these.

(c) Your date of birth. It is illegal for a company not to employ somebody because they are 'too young' or 'too old' – this is age discrimination. The information about your date of birth is irrelevant.

(d) Your gender. It does not matter what your gender is. Your employer is not allowed to give a job to a man just because they think that men are better than women at doing a particular job. This is also a form of discrimination.

(e) Your picture. Unless you are applying for a job as a model or TV presenter and the employer requires applicants to submit photos, pictures are not usually included in a CV.

The next two pages contain a made-up example of a skills-based CV. The author of this CV, John Smith, is a fresh graduate who would like to apply for a job in marketing. However, he does not have any experience in marketing. So, he has written a CV in which he emphasises his skills. Communication, teamwork and organisational skills are all vital for working in marketing. Therefore, John has looked at his work experience and found examples of effective communication, successful teamwork and good organisation. Later in this book, I will talk more about searching for such examples in your experience.

Let's look at the CV.

Mr John Smith[1]

Flat 2, 8 Anywhere Road, Anytown, AN1 5AB[2]
E-mail John.Daniel.Smith@gmail.com[3] **Tel.** 07987 654 321[4]

Education[5]

Anycity University 2013 – 2017[6]
BA English and Spanish, First Class Honours
A four-year course with an integrated study placement at the University of Malaga, Spain

Anytown Sixth Form College 2011 – 2013
A-levels: English (A); History (B); Spanish (A); Media Studies (A)

Skills[7]

Communication and Marketing Skills

- Planned and organised three successful charity bake sales with the Amnesty International Student Society; raised over £240[8] for the local Women's Crisis Centre;
- Created a presentation about Student Learning Mentor services at the Anycity University Library; delivered the presentation to over 800[9] students and increased attendance at the mentoring service;
- Wrote over 30[10] articles for Anycity University's Student Blog;

12

Teamwork and Organisational Skills

- Was appointed team leader for two group assignments (essay and presentation); successfully managed the workflow of the team, delivering excellent results – the mark for the entire team was over 70% for both assignments;
- Used to working both in a team and independently; amplified my skills of working independently and managing my time while working as a researcher at the English department of the University of Malaga;
- Excellent time management skills: successfully managed my studies while working part-time.

I.T. Skills

- MS Word – advanced; MS Excel – Intermediate; MS PowerPoint – Advanced;
- Outstanding internet research skills developed while working for the English department at the University of Malaga;
- Experience in blogging and internet publishing; familiar with most major blogging platforms;

Work Experience[11]

Researcher. The University of Malaga, English Department	**2015 – 2016**
Journalist. Anycity University Student Blog (voluntary)	**2013 – 2017**
Student Learning Mentor. Anycity University	**2014 – 2017**
Waiter and Cashier. Café Amelia, Anycity	**2013 – 2015**

13

Just like with Jane Smith's experience-based CV above, I will now provide an analysis of John Smith's skills-based CV.

Just like Jane Smith, John is also applying for a job in marketing. However, unlike Jane, he does not have any direct experience in marketing. Even his degree is not relevant to the job: Jane has a degree in Marketing and Management and John studied English and Spanish. However, he tried to extract as much as possible from his work experience and make his CV as relevant to the marketing position that he is applying for. Let's look at his CV in detail.

John's CV is one page long in this book because this is just an example. A real skills-based CV will be longer, more detailed, and contain more skills. Skills-based CVs are usually two pages long because CVs are written in response to job descriptions and these job descriptions usually contain a long list of skills that the candidate should have. It takes two pages to list examples and evidence of all the skills required from the candidate.

The purpose of a skills-based CV is to show how the applicant has acquired and developed all these skills over the course of his/her professional experience.

The first four elements of his CV are the same as Jane Smith's. However, number 5, Education, is a bit different.

5. Education. As you can see, John has added a bit more information about his education: he mentioned the fact that he did a four-year course with an integrated study placement abroad. Why did he mention it? Why is it relevant? Well, in the modern world it is important to have a global mindset and

having international experience, knowing an additional language and working in multi-national teams is always an advantage. If you have studied or worked abroad, it is definitely worth mentioning it on your CV.

7. Skills. The Skills section is the most important one in a CV. Even when you are writing an experience-based CV, you should highlight your skills: what skills you have developed while working in a particular position, what existing skills you have successfully applied in that job, etc. I will talk more about it in **Chapter 8: Presenting your Skills**.

In a skills-based CV, the skills are grouped into categories: John Smith tells the potential employer what skills he has and then gives examples and evidence of those skills.

8; 9; 10. Just like Jane Smith, John provides figures to make his evidence more specific and measureable. I would also like to draw your attention to the fact that sentences in both CVs presented above are incomplete: the subject is missing. When describing their work experience and skills, both John and Jane begin their sentences with verbs and not with the pronoun *I*. I will address this in more detail in **Chapter 11: The Language of the CV**.

11. Work Experience. Since none of the jobs John has held are relevant to the marketing position he is applying for, the work experience section of his skills-based CV goes at the end. In a two-page CV, it can go on the second page. The most important part of the CV is the Skills section.

Please note that, unlike in Jane Smith's experience-based CV, the Work Experience section in John's skills-based CV only contains the years when he worked in these positions, and not months. This is a little trick to make work experience seem more impressive. For example, John probably worked as a researcher at the University of Malaga from October 2015 to June 2016. However, when he only mentions the years and not the months, it appears that he stayed in this position over a year or maybe almost two years.

In the next chapter, I will talk more about the structure of the CV, the structure of this book, as well as about the elements that your CV *should* contain and *could* contain if you have space for them.

I would also like to note that in experience-based CVs almost all the jobs are usually more or less in the same field. For example, if you look at the CV of Jane Smith on pages 6-7 of this book, it becomes clear that she has worked mostly in the fields of marketing, promotions and events.

However, it can also happen that the jobs you have done over the course of your professional experience are not all in the same field. In this situation, these several lines that describe work responsibilities and achievements should make it relevant to the job you are applying for. For example, if you are applying for a job that requires good presentation skills and you want to list your job as a salesperson, you can emphasise the customer service, interpersonal and spoken communication skills, which are all related to giving presentations because a presenter must be friendly, positive and eloquent.

Chapter 2

Basic Elements of a CV

Let's start with the basics. So, once again, the purpose of your CV is to get you an interview, not a job. This means that you need to impress your potential employers and make them interested. This chapter talks about the elements CVs contain. Please note that not all CVs contain these elements: some are compulsory and some are optional. You only add them if you do not have much else to add. This usually happens if you are writing a skills-based CV and have too much information to make it one page long but not quite enough for two pages. However, most of these elements appear both on experience-based CVs and on skills-based ones.

Please also remember that you will need to write a CV in response to a job advertisement. These usually contain two documents: the job description and the person specification. Sometimes these two documents are combined into one. The job description usually contains a list of tasks and responsibilities that the job will involve; the person specification contains a list of skills and qualities that an ideal candidate for that job should have. The contents of your CV will depend on the job description and person specification. Therefore, you cannot send the same CV for different jobs in different fields: you will need to change it, a little or a lot, for each of the jobs for which you apply.

So, here are the main elements that CVs are made of, from the top to the bottom:

1. Your Name and Surname at the very top. Usually they are written in a larger font.

DO NOT write 'Curriculum Vitae' or 'CV' at the top of the document. Your potential employer knows that they are reading a CV. There is no need to tell them that.

About ten years ago, I was shown 'an example of how not to do it' – a three-page CV, the first page of which had the candidate's name, surname and the words 'Curriculum Vitae' printed in large red letters. And when I say 'large', I mean two-inch high. This looked like it was written by a person who had no idea what a CV should look like and had never seen one before. Nowadays, in the age of smartphones, information is literally at your fingertips. You just need to type 'CV example' into a search engine's search bar and you will be given thousands of great templates according to which you can write your CV. You can also use the examples from this book as I am using examples from CVs written by me and people I know, and all these examples got me and those people interviews.

2. Your contact details. These include your address and postcode, telephone number and email address.

3. Your Personal Profile. This section is optional. Some people are all for it; others advise against. Usually this section appears in skills-based CVs. I will write more about it in **Chapter 5: Personal Profile.**

4. Education. Here is your first chance to shine and stand out. See more in **Chapter 6: Education and How to Talk about It**.

5. Skills. Now this is the meat of the CV. In a skills-based CV, the Skills section precedes the Work Experience section. In an experience-based CV, the Skills section is much smaller: it only contains 'hard skills' such as languages, numeracy and IT and comes after the Work Experience section.

There are a range of skills that you can present, depending on the places where you've worked and the tasks you've performed. However, the main sets of skills are:

- Communication (spoken and written); this includes writing and presentation skills;

- Commercial awareness (knowing how businesses operate);

- Customer Service;

- Teamwork (all about co-operation and helping others);

- Planning and Organising;

- Motivation and Working on your own initiative;

- Information Technology and Computer Literacy (including internet-based research skills);

- Numeracy;

- Languages;

- Leadership – this one deserves a separate discussion and I will address this skill in **Chapter 8**. In short, a leader is not just someone who knows how to manage a team of people. A leader is someone who is able to spot a problem before anyone else does, and takes the necessary steps to solve it.

- Willingness to Learn.

Most of these skills will be on your CV (again, depending on the job description), and they will also be accompanied by specific examples and evidence demonstrating that you, indeed, possess them.

Chapter 8: Presenting Your Skills will deal with all of these in greater depth.

6. Work Experience. **Chapter 7: Work Experience and the Lack of It** will explain why you don't even need a job to build a great CV because it is enough to be *socially active* at university. However, if you do have a job or have had one in the past, either paid or unpaid, everything counts. Just mention the job title, the place of work, and the dates when you worked there. Your Skills section will tell your potential employer everything else.

7. Interests. This section is also optional – only include it if you have space. The most important thing is that your interests must be related to the job you're going to do. See **Chapter 9: Interests** for more information.

8. References available on request. This is another optional section. Some recruiters even advise against adding this sentence at the end of your CV because they see it as something to fill the blank space. It is much more useful to add a link to your professional blog if you have one.

9. A link to your LinkedIn profile. In case you are not aware of it, LinkedIn is a social media site for professionals. Think of it as Facebook for working people. Most of the updates, shared items and messages on that site are work-related. It is probably the best way to store your CV online. Unlike in a traditional CV, the space in which you write about your education and work experience is unlimited, so you can have a really well-rounded online profile.

10. Last but not least – an accompanying covering letter. Please see **Chapter 13: Covering Letter Tips** for information on covering letters – how to write them and how NOT to write them.

A lot of jobs nowadays do not require you to send a CV. Instead you need to fill out an application form. This is especially the case with university jobs (not only for teaching and research, but also for administrative and secretarial positions). However, the rules that apply to writing CVs also apply to application forms. **Chapter 14: How to Write Brilliant Application Forms** talks about this in detail.

This list is not exhaustive, but this is the most 'standard' set of elements that a CV contains. I will explain more about every one of those elements as we go along.

SPACE FOR YOUR NOTES

Chapter 3

The S.M.A.R.T. CV

Before we start dealing with the specifics, I would like to describe a general principle of writing CVs, covering letters and application forms, which is called a SMART approach. SMART is an acronym that is widely used in self-help literature. In this book the meaning of the acronym SMART is:

S – Specific

M – Measurable

A – Achievement-oriented

R – Relevant

T – Traceable (and Truthful)

Let's briefly analyse all of them one by one.

S – Specific

Being specific means providing details instead of talking in general terms. In order for your CV to be as convincing as possible, you have to give the details about your achievements and responsibilities at work, answering these questions: *What? When? Where? How much? Who?* When describing your education, skills, accomplishments and work experience, please give the details: dates, places, projects, numbers, etc.

Let me give you an example. If you simply write that you have great teamwork skills, your employer might wonder if you really do have them. However, if you provide evidence for this, it looks much more impressive and convincing.

Let us look how John Smith describes his teamwork skills in his skills-based CV.

- *Planned and organised three successful charity bake sales with the Amnesty International Student Society; raised over £240 for the local Women's Crisis Centre;*
- *Was appointed team leader for two group assignments (essay and presentation); successfully managed the workflow of the team, delivering excellent results – the mark for the entire team was over 70% for both assignments;*

As you can see, he is very specific: he mentions what kind of teams he was working with, what they were doing and what the result of the successful team work was (£240 raised and marks over 70%).

You also need to be specific when you mention your work experience. When you write a skills-based CV, you only need to write the job title, the dates and the organisation. When you write an experience-based CV, it is important to list your responsibilities and achievements. Let us look at the example below.

Secretary/Events Officer

Anycity University Volleyball society 2012-2013

- *Organising official and social events, tournaments. Organised ten inter-university competitions.*

- *Managing a Facebook community page. Increased the society's social media exposure by uploading videos and photos from training sessions and tournaments;*

The person who wrote this focuses on specific achievements: organised ten competitions; increased the society's social media exposure.

M – Measurable

This is all about the facts and figures. Your results and achievements should be measurable. Let's look at the examples:

- *Managed student teams for three university assignments with close deadlines. The teams received first class marks for 2 assignments out of 3.*
- *Organised an inter-university conference on green technology, involving 10 speakers from 3 universities.*

As you can see from the above, achievements are measured and illustrated with figures. This is what you should do, too.

A – Achievement-oriented

This is perfectly straightforward. Spend as little time as possible describing your duties and day-to-day activities, and focus on your achievements instead. And by the way, do not call them duties – they are called *responsibilities*!

Even in an experience-based CV, the majority of your job description in the work experience section will be about your achievements. When you start writing your CV, do not think about the length, about one or two pages – write as many pages as you can, as much as you can about every job and position of responsibility you have held. Write what skills you have developed, what projects you have accomplished and what rewards you got for it. Provide figures and facts – it will help you impress your prospective employer. Next, look at the job description and person specification again and edit your CV so that only the most relevant information remains. However, before you edit, you should have as much information about your professional path as possible.

I cannot emphasise it more:

WRITE DOWN EVERY SINGLE ACHIEVEMENT, NO MATTER HOW SMALL! You will use all that information later – when preparing for interviews, when writing another CV, when filing in application forms, etc.

And then, when you edit your CV, make all your achievements look big and important. Because there are no small achievements. They are all yours. And they are all important. They all make you what you are and contribute to your professional and personal development. They make you better – every single one of them.

Let me give you an example. Imagine that you are writing a skills-based CV for an internship, a work placement or a graduate position, and you want to describe your job in a fast-food restaurant in that CV. You could say that all you did was serving food and taking money, but that does not say much about you to your potential employer. However, let us see how your experience in the restaurant can be turned into achievements:

- *Boosted my teamwork and self-motivation skills while working in a fast-paced environment (a fast food restaurant);*

- *Developed excellent customer service skills: served over 200 customers per day; received positive feedback on my service from my supervisors;*

- *Successfully applied my numerical skills while working on the till; was responsible for cash handling and depositing the revenue for the day into the safe;*

See what I've done here? Everything you do can lead to the development of skills and to achievements. What matters is how you present your experience.

R – Relevant

I will repeat this several times throughout this book. Your CV must be relevant. It must correspond to the job for which you're applying. You would not write about your skills in photography if you are applying for a job as an investment banker, would you? However, being skilled in photography is beneficial if you are applying to work as a designer or a marketing professional (photographs can be used to produce marketing collateral).

It's very simple – look at the keywords in the job advertisement and the job description and make your CV reflect those keywords. Make sure that your CV contains information about the experience and skills that they want the candidates to have. If you are applying speculatively (i.e. sending the same CV to 100 companies for the same position in case they have a vacancy), then read what the position normally entails and what skills you need for it. One of the best sites to find this kind of information (what qualifications and skills you need to do a particular job) is www.prospects.ac.uk.

T – Traceable (and Truthful)

This means only one thing: do not invent stuff. Do not lie. I would like to make myself clear: if you take a small achievement and make it look important, that is not lying. That is presenting a true event, a true achievement and using powerful words while doing it. Lying is writing about achievements that do not exist.

Just write what you have done. Even if it is not very easy to check whether a company/student society exists, the employer might ask you additional questions about that non-existent experience during the interview. Do you really want your employer to see how you are sweating and how your eyes are darting from one side to another as you are trying to invent a story on the spot? Quite honestly, it's not worth it. It won't be fun if you're found out. In short, if you lie – prepare to say goodbye.

Chapter 4

The Beginning: Looking Professional

As the saying goes, you will never have a second chance to make the first impression. The first impression is also the last one. This means that your CV must look professional. There are several things you need to consider and all of them are equally important.

Why? Because employers will give your CV about 20 seconds. At most. Recruiters, head-hunters and human resource managers receive scores of CVs every day, if not hundreds. This means that you have to capture their attention and make it easy for them to read. If they see you have not bothered to ensure that, they will not bother to read it. Period.

There is a joke among recruiters. They say that they put CVs into two piles: pile A and pile B. The B stands for 'Bin'.

There's something else: human resources professionals are overworked. What does it mean to you? It means that you'll have to write your CV in a way that is very easy to read (they read CVs all day, so have mercy on their eyes) and to understand (they read CVs all day, some of them written very badly, so have mercy on their brains). Here are some tips on how to make it easy for the recruiters.

1. Keep it simple. No fancy fonts. 12 point, Times New Roman, Arial or the like. One-inch (2.5 cm) margins.

Some of you may argue with me about this point. You may ask: *But what about uniqueness and standing out? I don't want my CV to look like everyone else's!*

Yes, standing out is important. However, if you want to create an original CV, it is only acceptable for jobs where such creativity is valued. You can find plenty of articles online about original CV designs, such as printed on a t-shirt, one that looks like the front page of a newspaper or like a box which you need to open to find the information about the candidate inside. These CVs are not for economists, accountants or lawyers – rather, they are for designers and artists and they showcase the candidates' professional skills.

However, you can make a 'classical', conservative CV stand out from the pile of others by printing it on thicker paper (it can even be a pale shade of yellow or blue). You can also play with the layout using tabs, bullet points, lines, section dividers, etc. This will also make it easier to read – and you DO want to make your recruiter's job easy. They appreciate that.

2. Do not write CURRICULUM VITAE at the top. I had to repeat this one because many people still make the mistake. Your name and surname (e.g. *Mr John Smith* or *Ms Jane Smith*) typed in a larger font (size 16-18, could be **bold**) is more than enough.

3. Make your section headings stand out. Look at the CVs of John Smith (pp. 12-13) and Jane Smith (pp. 6-7). Every section is divided by a horizontal line and every heading is in bold. The names of the sections (Education, Work Experience,

Skills) are bold, underlined and placed in the centre of the page. All of this makes the CV easier to read.

3. Do not provide an autobiography. Focus on what the recruiter needs to know. He/she needs to know if you have the qualities that were specified in the job advertisement. So stick to that and make sure you mention what is required.

Having said that, as I advised you before, when you start writing your CV, you are allowed to write everything you can think of and make it more than two pages long. You can edit it afterwards.

4. Divide it into sections and label them clearly. Make it as obvious as possible that THIS section is about your education and THAT ONE is about your skills.

5. As mentioned before, keep your email address professional. The one you created when you were fourteen is most likely not suitable for a CV, so take the time to set up a professional email account. Emails like *hotstuff_69@mail.com* and *I_AM_IRON_MAN@mailbox.co.uk* do not inspire confidence or give a sense of professionalism. Use your university email or just set up an account with your name before the @ sign (e.g. j.d.smith@yahoo.com).

6. Proofread your CV. Have a friend read it, too. Nothing screams 'Pile B!' than spelling and grammar mistakes. Your CV may go into the bin straight away.

7. Do not mix up your tenses. This rule usually applies when you are writing an experience-based CV and describing your responsibilities in the jobs that you have held. Write what you DID in past tense (e.g. for past jobs) and what you

are DOING NOW in present tense (e.g. your current job). Sounds obvious, but it is a pretty common mistake.

8. Avoid clichés. Do not use words like 'think outside the box', or 'team player' etc. See **Chapter 10: CV Clichés to Be Avoided like the Plague** to find out which phrases are overused in CVs and therefore frowned upon.

9. As mentioned before, do not include a photo unless you are applying for a job as a model, actor/actress, TV presenter or any other job where your face will be seen by millions *and* the job description asks you to submit a photo.

10. Have a clean social media profile. This means two things. First of all, register on LinkedIn. This website allows you to develop professional relationships and to showcase your work experience and skills. Secondly, go over your other social media accounts (Facebook, Twitter, Instagram, etc.) with a fine-tooth comb and remove all pictures and posts that could be considered unprofessional or controversial. More and more often, employers search for information about the candidates online. This means that you should remove all pictures from parties, all pictures where people are drinking and in which you are also tagged (even if you are not drinking in those pictures), all posts that contain strong language, etc. Basically, if you think that it might be unprofessional, it probably is. Remove it.

In short, you should make your CV look good. It has to be love at first sight for your prospective employers. After all, your CV is your face. Just as you would not arrive to a job interview in a dirty suit, do not send in a sloppy CV.

Chapter 5

Personal Profile

A personal profile is a very brief summary of your education, skills and (possibly) your work experience. It can be included both in experience-based and skills-based CVs, but usually a one-page CV is too short for it. It is used by experienced professionals who have a long work history and can write a two-page experience-based CV and by those who write skill-based CVs. In both cases, the personal profile appears at the top of the CV, just under the contact details, before the Education section.

When you write a personal profile for your CV, you really need to know what to include there. In some recruitment agencies, especially if they receive a lot of CVs per day, CVs are often scanned using software that looks for specific keywords (usually those mentioned in the job description of the position for which you are applying). One of the functions of a personal profile is to contain those keywords that automatic scanners will detect. However, it is important to include those keywords in your CV even if it does not contain the profile section. In this case, the keywords go in the Work Experience and/or Skills sections.

So, what should a personal profile consist of? And what should it look like? Here are some tips:

1. Make it short – 120 words is the upper limit. Anywhere between 60 and 80 is fine.

2. Do not use 'I' – write about yourself in the third person.

3. 1-2 keywords in a sentence. Not more.

4. You do not necessarily need to provide evidence and examples in the profile section. Just list the skills and the qualities, whatever the job description requires. You will add the specific examples later, in your Work Experience or Skills section.

5. If you have enough space on the CV (two pages) make it 1.1 or 1.15 line spaced. It will be easier to read. For example, in this book, 1.1 line spacing is used.

6. List your special achievements. Mention your education and key skills. Three is the magic number, so list the main three skills/sets of skills at most.

7. Mention your career aim. This information should go in the first sentence: write briefly about yourself and your career objectives.

8. VERY IMPORTANT: Modify it with every different job you apply to. Match it with the job profile. This, as I mentioned before, applies to the entire CV. Sending the same CV to one hundred different companies will not get you anywhere unless all of them have identical job descriptions.

9. Read it aloud to see if it reads well. Have a friend proofread the profile. After all, it is the first thing your future employer sees when they look at your CV.

10. If space is precious, omit the profile altogether. You will have enough of a chance to impress your employers in the Education and Skills sections. If you do not include the profile, mention the keywords in the body of the CV.

Examples:

Mr John Smith (72 words)

A student of Politics and International Relations at the Anycity University with strong commercial and political awareness (member of the Economics society) and outstanding communication skills (18 months experience as a student journalist and secretary of the Debate Club) looking for an internship in public relations in an NGO. A keen learner, flexible, willing to apply his knowledge and learn new skills with a view to establishing himself in the NGO sector.

Ms Jane Smith (84 words)

A recent graduate of Business and French (2:1 honours degree from Anycity University) with experience of project and events management (secretary of the Karate Society for 3 years) as well as strong interest in recruitment (increased the number of the French Society members by 200%; the largest Language Society of the past five years). Looking for opportunities in the field of human resources. Experience abroad (HR intern at L'Oreal Paris). Dissertation topic: Employee Retention Strategies in Fashion Retail Businesses in the UK and France.

As you can see, I am breaking rule number four in these examples: I do back claims about skills with evidence. This is also possible. You are allowed to get creative in your personal profile section. It also depends on how much experience you have and what your profile wants to highlight.

The examples above are, in fact, very short – well below the upper limit of 120 words. However, they illustrate one of the main ideas of this book: work experience and competencies can be found in any student activity. It is important to realise that you have to take advantage of those activities – especially in your first and second years of university. I talk more about becoming more employable at while you are doing your degree in my book *Fight for that Job! How to become employable while you are still at university.*

Here is another example from a CV written by me, which got me an interview. It was a CV written for a communications position in a university, shortly after my graduation. Its length is 89 words.

A first-class graduate with a wealth of experience in writing, marketing, project management, communications and promotional work, looking for a position in a higher education setting that would help me make a valuable contribution with my education, knowledge of the student market and the education sector, work experience, professional skills and personal qualities.

Excellent written and spoken communication skills (including presentation skills), organisational abilities, knowledge of representation, promotional work and relationship-building, ability to work both in a team and independently, and great analytical skills developed through diverse work experience.

Chapter 6

Education and How to Talk about It

There are several ways to describe your education in a CV. If you finished your degree a long time ago (I mean more than 2 years ago) and have had some work experience since then, it is enough to list the university, the academic subject, the years and the degree classification (First, 2.1, 2.2, etc.). However, if you are still studying or have just finished your degree, it is also worth listing some of your educational achievements. If you are writing a one-page CV, your education section will be small. However, one-page CVs are mostly experience-based. If your CV is two pages long, then it's worth investing a bit more in a detailed description of your academic path – not of what you have done, but how well you've done it. Having said that, I must repeat that you should only make the Education section of your CV longer if you have space for it. Normally this will be the case when you are writing a skills-based CV. If you do not have space, keep it short and write more for the Skills section.

What to mention in your education section:

University Education

1. The obvious parts: Degree title, name of the university, years (start and (projected) finish). If you still studying, it is a

good idea to state just under this information which year you are in and your predicted final grade.

NB: Start with the most recent education. Your university degree is more important than your A-levels and your A-levels are more important than your GCSEs.

2. If you are not in your first year of studies, then also write the average grade for your first year (if you're proud of it). If you are currently in your first year, I would like to say that you should not believe the myth that first year grades do not count and all you need to do is pass the year (get 40% for all of the assignments). Yes, maybe your first year grades do not count towards your final degree classification, but they definitely do count towards your employability.

Imagine that you are applying for a summer internship at the end of your first year. Or even a work placement at the start of your second year. Your grades speak volumes about you to your potential employer because they show how hard-working you are and how serious you are about everything you do. Your employer is going to judge how hard you will work based on how hard you study. If your average grade for the first year is 43%, your employer might think that you are just a party animal who does not care too much about his/her degree, doing the bare minimum of work needed to pass, and therefore might have the same attitude towards the job.

3. Modules/subjects in which you are specialising or for which you received a good grade (if relevant to the job). If you don't want your employer to see all your grades, write only the best ones. Emphasise your achievements and small

victories. I would also like to add right from the start that for some jobs, it might be useful to mention your grades if the subjects you have studied are relevant to the job for which you are applying. For example, if you are applying for a job that requires good numerical skills, the fact that you have a GCSE or an A-level in Mathematics should be mentioned, especially if the grade is good. If your essays and/or reports are especially good and the job requires excellent written communication skills, put on your CV that you are skilled in research and writing.

Examples:

Mr John Smith who is in his second year is applying for an internship in a bank:

BSc Marketing and Management. Anycity University. 2016 – Present

- *Currently in 2nd year – First Class predicted. Av. grade for1st year – 75%;*

- *Excellent numerical skills: First Class passes in Mathematics (87%) and Business Decision Analysis (76%);*

- *Successfully applied my research and written communication skills while undertaking written assignments. Grades for essays: Organisational Psychology – 75%; Principles of Marketing – 72%;*

Ms Jane Smith, a second-year student, is applying for a job as a part-time secretary.

BA English Language. Anycity University. 2016 – Present .

- *Currently in 2nd year, First Class predicted. Average grade for the first year – 73%;*
- *Demonstrated excellent time management skills by successfully combining full-time studies and volunteering;*
- *Outstanding written communication and research skills, demonstrated by first-class grades for academic essays;*
- *Excellent computer literacy skills. Grade for the module 'ITC for Language Analysis' – 79%.*

In short, although in a skills-based CV your skills are the centre of attention, you should also spend some time working your Education section. As you can see, both John and Jane highlight the subjects and the grades that demonstrate that the candidate has the skills needed for doing a particular job. John emphasises his numerical and written communication skills that are needed for working in a bank; Jane highlights her organisational, communication and IT skills needed for secretarial work.

You can add the following details:

4. Any academic awards or special achievements (for example, some universities and departments give awards to the best first-year students). If you happen to have obtained one, well done to you! Definitely list it on your CV. Generally, the rule is: if you've got it, flaunt it!

A-levels

It is worth mentioning the results of your grades from the final year of school (A-levels in your case), what subjects you studied and what examinations you took. However, anything else is not really relevant anymore There will come a time when you have so much experience that even school exams won't be relevant, but for now let's keep them – after all, it's been so little time since you sat them.

GCSEs (To Put or Not to Put?)

If you have already finished your degree, you should probably just mention your university education and A-levels, as well as your grades. If you are studying for a postgraduate degree (Master's or PhD), then even your A-levels may not be that relevant anymore.

However, if you are still studying for an undergraduate degree and there is space in your CV, you can mention your GCSEs. Yet, you do not have to list every single one of them – just write how many A-C grades you have. An important point is that you do not have to mention your grades if you are not proud of them. If you do not really want to disclose your GCSE grades, you can simply write how many GCSEs you have passed. Many jobs require you to have passed GCSE Mathematics and English, you can mention those, or their equivalents from your country.

SPACE FOR YOUR NOTES

Chapter 7

Work Experience and the Lack of It

How do you present your work experience? This short chapter will tell you all about it.

In a skills-based CV, your Work Experience section does not take much space. Each job must take no more than 2-3 lines. Sometimes (like in the CV of John Smith on pages 12-13) it is only one line. The format is the following: job title, company, times and briefly the responsibilities – if you have space. As you can see, the example CV of John Smith does not contain responsibilities. However, if your CV is two pages long, you can fit them in there. As a rule, the responsibilities should not take more than two lines, three at most.

Consider the following examples:

Journalist

Anycity University Herald　　　　*October 2012 – June 2015*

Writing articles on everyday student issues. Responsible for graphic design, editing and proofreading.

Fundraiser

Amnesty International Student Society October 2014 – March 2015
Organised more than 10 events and charity sales to raise money for local charities.

Communications Officer

Tae Kwon Do Society   2013 – 2015
Managed a social network of 60 members of the society. Organised inter-university competitions.

You get the idea. Follow the KISS principle – Keep It Short and Simple. Your responsibilities in your work history are important, of course, but not as important as the skills that you have acquired or your work-related achievements.

Job titles are another thing that is not very important. What matters much more are your achievements, what you have done with your time while you were doing that job (whether paid or voluntary).

Let me put it straight for you:

Any activity, anything you do while at university, can count as work experience. The only thing you have to do is be active in that position. The rest will be easy.

In the next chapter, I will talk about presenting your skills – the indispensable practical competencies that you will have developed throughout your working and academic life.

Chapter 8

Presenting Your Skills

As mentioned before, the main thing about your Skills section (the most important one in the skills-based CV) is bringing your greatest achievements into the spotlight. The list of your skills is worthless if it is not backed up with examples and evidence. Those examples have to be concrete, measurable and well-worded. They have to be S.M.A.R.T. (see **Chapter 3**). They must demonstrate that you know what you're talking about and that you reflect upon what you're doing. They have to answer the following questions: **What? Where? Why? When? Who?** and **How much?**

Below is the list you have already seen in Chapter 2.

These skills are more general and can appear in almost everyone's CV:

- Communication (spoken and written);

- Commercial Awareness

- Customer Service;

- Teamwork;

- Planning and Organising;

- Leadership;

- Motivation and Working on your own initiative;

- Willingness to Learn;

The following skills are more specific and will be discussed separately:

- Research;
- Information Technology and Computer Literacy;
- Numeracy;
- Languages.

Let's break all of those down and understand how they have to be presented on your CV.

Naturally, you do not have to list all of those skills. As mentioned before, you need to tailor your CV according to the job description. However, the most important aspect of presenting your skills is presenting evidence that can somehow be measured.

Please look at the examples below and see how facts and figures, concrete names of organisations, etc. have been skilfully woven into the text. Note, however, that these are merely examples and that they are provided for inspiration. If your experience is different, just use them as templates.

1. Communication

This is all about reaching out to people – persuading, arguing, informing, negotiating, presenting, etc. Here are a few examples of how those can appear on your CV:

Communication Skills

- *Active member of the Public Speaking Club. Elected Speaker of the Week 3 times this year;*
- *Six presentations on Academic Writing given to sixth form students at Anytown College and Anycity University;*
- *Street fundraising: raised over £1000 for the Raise and Give society Cancer Research Support programme.*

2. Customer Service

Those are the skills that you will have developed having worked in any service sector job. Look at the examples below:

Customer Service Skills:

- *Amplified customer service skills whilst working as a bartender at Anycity University Pub. Key competences: efficiency under pressure, multi-tasking and excellent face-to face and telephone manner;*
- *Boosted sales and customer service skills whilst working at The Bookworm Bookstore. Key competences: link sales, excellent telephone manner, knowledge of stock.*

3. Teamwork

Teamwork is all about co-operation, helping others, managing conflicts and sharing responsibility for successes and failures. Here's what you could write:

Teamwork Skills:

- *Amplified teamwork skills throughout my academic and professional life: active member of Anycity University Football Club; regularly organising study groups in preparation for examinations;*
- *Managed teams for three group assignments. The groups got first class passes for two essays and a presentation;*
- *Actively involved in a team of volunteers on Anycity Queen's Park conservation project;*
- *Worked in a team with the Investment Society to organise The Undergraduate Traders' Conference at Anycity University (over 120 participants, 8 speakers).*

4. Planning and Organising

These skills are all about time management and ability to multi-task. They can be presented this way:

Organisational Skills:

- *Successfully combined studies with part-time employment and participation in student societies; average grade for the first and second years – 72%;*
- *Managed the Facebook page for the University Football Team. Organised society events, preseason games, inter-university competitions and social gatherings.*

5. Motivation and Working on Your Own Initiative

This is very simple – mention anything you have started by yourself and accomplished either on your own, or with the help of a team that you had engaged in the task.

6. Willingness to Learn

This skill – or should I say 'trait' – is crucial for a modern employee. It shows that you are open-minded, open to new experiences and are willing to take up a new challenge. For instance, this is another example from my CV. I hold a degree in International Relations and English Language. However, I undertook a work placement as a Communications Officer in a science research council. Here is how I describe it:

Having come from a non-scientific background, showed diligence and motivation and learnt on the job whilst working for a science research council.

7. Leadership

The skill of leadership is an interesting one. It is not only about leading a team of people and managing things from above. Sometimes you might not even know you have it. It might be disguised as initiative, willingness to go the extra mile. I would like to write about two examples of leadership where my manager noticed that this was leadership and I thought that it was simply initiative.

1. When I was working as a Communications Officer for Amnesty International Student Society, we organised a charity bake sale at the university pub. During the sale, I noticed that there were not that many customers coming to our stand. Then I decided to take initiative and take the baked goods to the tables, asking people if they would like to buy cupcakes for charity. I also encouraged the team to do the same. The strategy worked and the sales moved much faster.

We sold all our stock within an hour of implementing the idea and raised over £100 for charity.

2. When I was working as a writing mentor in the library of my university, I noticed that there was not a lot of demand for our service. I saw this as a triple problem. First of all, our writing mentors were not getting the experience they needed and often waited in vain. Secondly, our students were not benefitting from the service. Thirdly, the continued funding of the scheme depended on the demonstration of results and low demand meant fewer results that the writing mentor centre could present. I analysed the situation and saw that awareness of our services was the problem. I engaged a team of mentors to design a presentation on our services. Then I delivered the presentation to over 800 students at the university. As a result, the student awareness was increased and we were fully booked until the end of the academic year.

The two examples above show evidence of several skills. (1) Teamwork – engaging a team of people to achieve my goals; (2) Analysis – noticing a problem and analysing its causes; (3) Initiative – being the one to take initiative to solve the problem; (4) Problem-solving – taking certain steps to overcome the challenge; (5) Communication skills – using them to achieve my objectives: to sell the baked goods and to increase the students' awareness of the writing mentor service; (6) Motivating myself and others.

In a way, the skill of leadership is a combination of multiple skills that employers require the candidates to have.

Of course, the examples I have given here, in their current form, cannot be put on a CV. Their format allows them to be used only in a job interview situation. They have been provided merely for illustration purposes.

8. Job-specific skills

The other five sets of skills (Research, Information Technology and Computer Literacy, Numeracy, Languages and Commercial Awareness) are job-specific. Languages and IT are more universal – they can be useful in any job, so you should mention your language competencies (native, fluent, intermediate, conversational) and describe your IT skills (Microsoft Office, Internet-based research, programming, knowledge of specialist software, etc.) in greater detail on your CV.

Research skills are all about seeking and finding information. This includes using the search engines to find information, as well as reviewing literature for your assignments. As a student, you will have plenty of opportunities to develop those and to provide examples in your CV.

Although I put the skill of Commercial Awareness into the job-specific group, on second thoughts it is also a skill needed in almost every job. Commercial Awareness is basic knowledge of how businesses operate – demand, supply, marketing, customer relations and the creation of relationships that lead to sales. It also involves understanding the industry in which you are hoping to work. It is mostly commons sense, but I would advise to research your industry well when you apply for jobs. Please see the links and QR codes below to read more literature on this skill.

City University London (2013). *Developing Commercial Awareness* [online]. Available at: goo.gl/GFsusn

The University of Birmingham (2014). *A Guide to Commercial Awareness* [Online]. Available at: goo.gl/eVaRi7

Chapter 9

Interests

This brief chapter deals with the Interests section of your CV. It is not a compulsory section, so add it only if you have space for it. What interest of yours can you put in the CV? What is your employer interested in? Well, here it is:

1. In the majority of cases, your employer does not care what books you've read and what music you like.

2. They do not care which countries you have visited during your backpacking trips.

3. This means that your interests have to be professionally oriented.

4. For example – if you're applying for a job in banking, then write that you are interested in economics and mention the publications you regularly read. If you are applying for a job in a museum and your degree is not in history, then write you're interested in history and demonstrate this – for example, through a membership in a professional society, participation in specialised conferences and events, etc. These principles can be used in all areas of work.

Do not forget to provide examples with concrete facts and figures that demonstrate your interests are genuine and not made-up!

4. (VERY IMPORTANT!) Do not include socialising into your list of interests.

5. ...yes, even if it is the case!

6. Because in the employers' language it means drinking.

7. Make it concrete and specific. Do not write 'travelling'. Write 'Backpacked in Latin America for 4 months'. Keep the S.M.A.R.T. scheme in mind. If you did some volunteering along the way, even better – definitely do mention it.

8. Sports are a great addition to your list of interests. That means any sports. Team sports show that you have teamwork skills; individual sports show that you are dedicating your time to self-improvement. Either way, even individual sports are done in a sports club where you can develop a range of skills, including teamwork.

9. OK, you are allowed to include personal interests too. It does not have to be exclusively professional. You're not a robot. But do not write 'reading and travelling' because everyone else writes it too. It's boring and has become a cliché. 'Climbing, gardening and cooking' sounds much more interesting – as long as it is true, of course. At least, you will have a point of interest to talk about at the interview!

Chapter 10

CV Clichés to Be Avoided Like the Plague!

There are some over-used phrases that can really make your CV look dull and give your potential employer an impression that you simply copy-pasted something your found online. They are known as clichés. Here are some of the most common ones:

- Excellent communication skills

- Strong work ethic

- Hard worker

- Good team player

- Results oriented

What is the problem with them?

They do not say anything useful about you! Of course, you want to make sure everyone knows how great you are, but your claims are not backed up with specific examples. They are too general. In short – THEY DO NOT MAKE YOU STAND OUT! They do not make you look interesting.

Thus, the main purpose of the CV fails.

I have already listed some examples of how you can present your successes (See **Chapters 7 and 8**).

There are also a few words that you should never put on your CV. The text below has been adapted from http://www.youtern.com/.

1. Approximately

Why do you have to approximate? You don't know what you did? Or you do know, but creating a good first impression wasn't a big priority for you when the resume was sent to the employer? If you don't know – find out. If you do know – show some confidence, and tell your potential employer exactly what you accomplished, with exact facts and figures. Make it look impressive! The word 'approximately' is not impressive.

A point of advice: write "over" or "more than". Forget approximation if it is not to the larger side. For example, I wrote in my CVs: *delivered presentations on academic writing to more than 800 students; produced over 40 articles about high-tech businesses at the science campus;*

2. Assisted

Unless you work in a dental office or are a point guard, employers do not want to hear about your 'assists'. Employers want you to demonstrate leadership skills, so they want to know that you were the one being assisted. In a humble way, tell them what you did, how you did it, and if you led a team, how many people were involved in the process.

A point of advice: Instead of writing 'assisted', write 'actively co-operated/collaborated/liaised with the executive team as as ... [add job title]. Achieved A, B and C'.

As mentioned before, a leader is not necessarily a team manager. A leader is someone who can spot a problem before anybody else does and manage to fix it, either by themselves or put a team together that will do it. A leader will also be a part of that team and work alongside everyone else.

3. Attempted

Never, ever tell your potential employer what you wanted to do. Instead, confidently tell them what you did, including a quantitative statement (facts and figures that allow your achievement to be measured). Good examples: "Increased customer satisfaction by 47%[2]" and "Exceeded the sales targets by an average of 7.5% every quarter"

A point of advice: make it sound powerful and complete! Do not give an impression of incomplete work. The word 'attempted', or even 'aimed' or 'tried' creates the impression that you tried but failed.

4. Team player

Recruiters like team players; they really do. However, can you not find a creative way to demonstrate that you are, indeed, a team player? For instance, you could say that you take great pride in being a mentor; that your team with whom you were doing a university assignment had achieved excellent results because of the

---

[2] I am not quite sure how customer satisfaction is measured, but I think they take some kind of satisfaction surveys and compare the average score (on the scale of one to ten). It can also be done by comparing the number of 'very satisfied' and 'satisfied' responses for each month.

way you organised things. Or maybe you took initiative while volunteering or fundraising and achieved good results? Anything but 'team player'. Recruiters need examples and evidence, not empty statements.

5. Professional

Is anyone going to admit they were less-than-professional during their previous jobs? In your career, being professional is a given, just like breathing. It's an empty word. There are better ways to describe professionalism: sound interpersonal skills, excellent customer service, outstanding time management and organisational skills, etc.

A point of advice: **Professionalism can be proven with examples. You will write plenty of those in your Skills, Education and Work Experience sections. If you have the word *professional* in your CV, delete it. Replace it with other phrases that show your potential employer that you are a professional.**

6. Hopefully

Today's economy is tough. There is a lot of competition for jobs and recruiters understand that people are hungry for work – and are just hoping for a chance to show what they can do. Do yourself a favour, however: remove this word!

A point of advice: **'Hopefully' sounds weak and implies doubt. What recruiters would really like to see in your CV is more certainty and confidence. Perhaps the only place where you can use the word *hope* is in an email or a covering letter** where you write, 'I hope to hear from you soon'. However, 'I am readily available for an interview and I am looking forward to hearing from you soon' sounds more powerful and more confident.

SPACE FOR YOUR NOTES

Chapter 11

The Language of the CV

The language of your CV is as vital as the presentation. Here are several tips for powerful, impact-making CVs:

1. Proofread it. First do it yourself and then have a friend look at it.

Sounds obvious, but grammar mistakes are treacherous. Moreover, they are a massive turn-off for the employers and recruiters. Check it. Put it away for a bit. Then re-check it.

2. Use telegraphic speech.

A CV is a document that gets read fast, for a very short amount of time. You have to get to the essence so don't be too verbose. Cut your sentences. Remove the subjects from the sentences (the word *I* in this case). Use bullet-points.

Bad (can pass in the covering letter, but not in a CV):

During my studies I worked as an events officer for the Anycity University's Drama Society. I organised social and cultural events, invited local theatre groups for workshops and collaboration, which positively impacted our performance skills and as a result, we produced two successful shows.

Good:

- *Organised six workshops conducted by theatre professionals for Anycity University Drama Society.*

- *Result — overall performance improvement and two successful productions*

- *£1000 pounds raised for charity from production-related sales and merchandise.*

3. Use positive, powerful verbs

It is important to use powerful-sounding verbs in your CV. For example, you can say that you *developed, boosted, magnified, amplified* your skills. You can write that you *worked together with someone* but you can also *collaborate, co-operate closely, liaise actively*, etc.

This list has been adapted from http://resumizer.com/action_verbs.htm. It is a long one, but a good one nonetheless.

NB: Remember that none of these words will work without specific examples!

Achieve
Acted as
Active in
Adapt
Administer
Advice
Allocate
Analyse
Anticipate
Approve
Arrange
Assess
Attend
Balance
Budget
Calculate
Chaperone
Clarify

Coach
Communicate
Compare
Complete
Conduct
Construct
Consult
Control
Cooperate
Coordinate
Counsel
Create
Decide
Define
Delegate
Demonstrate
Design
Determine

Diagnose
Direct
Discipline
Discover
Display
Distribute
Document
Draft
Earn
Edit
Eliminate
Employ
Enact
Encourage
Enforce
Enhance
Establish
Evaluate

Examine
Express
Facilitate
Follow up
Formulate
Gain
Generate
Grade
Guide
Handle
Identify
Illustrate
Implement
Improve
Improvise
Incorporate
Increase
Influence

Inform
Initiate
Inspect
Inspire
Instruct
Integrate
Interact
Interpret
Interview
Investigate
Involve
Judge
Lead
Lecture
Liaise
Locate
Maintain
Manage

Mediate
Modify
Monitor
Motivate
Negotiate
Observe
Obtain
Operate
Order
Organise
Originate
Oversee
Participate
Perceive
Perform
Plan
Predict
Prepare

Prescribe
Present
Prevent
Produce
Propose
Prove
Provide
Publicise
Publish
Question
Realise
Recognise
Recommend
Redesign
Refer
Reinforce
Relate

Reorganise
Report
Represent
Research
Resolve
Review
Revise
Schedule
Screen
Select
Serve
Simplify
Solve
Speak
Standardise
Stimulate
Strengthen

Structure
Substitute
Summarise
Supervise
Support
Teach
Test
Train
Transform
Translate
Treat
Tutor
Utilise
Verify
Win
Write

SPACE FOR YOUR NOTES

Chapter 12

CV Writing as a WRITING Process

As a writer, I just felt I had to add this little chapter.

You see, in writing a CV the key word is WRITING. As a writer, I must tell you that NO first draft is perfect. Even if it is almost perfect, the key word is ALMOST. When I was writing this book, I had to revise it several times, coming back to each chapter over and over before I considered it worthy of publication. I did not want to give you, my readers, something of bad quality. You do not want to give the same to your potential employer.

Roald Dahl, a British children's writer, once said that he went through forty (!) drafts before sending his books to press. Children are the most critical readers and they sense bad quality really well. Employers and recruiters are the most critical readers after the children. This means only one thing: a CV must be revised, proofread and edited several times before it can be submitted.

Here are some tips on writing and re-writing:

1. Write ALL YOU CAN about your education, skills, work experience, membership in societies, brilliant grades, volunteering and everything else you can think of.

2. Yes, it can be 10 pages long in the beginning.

3. Save and close the long document you have just created. Send it to yourself by email. Then back it up on a USB stick and on your phone. And, just in case, in a couple of other places. Save it as a Word document (.doc) and as a PDF, too. Why? Because Word documents may not look the same on two different computers. If someone has different settings on their word processing software, your neatly formatted two-page CV might turn into a three-page document with a single line on the third page. I am not even talking about the difficulties caused by documents created on an Apple computer when you try to open them on a Microsoft computer.

Therefore, when you send your CV and covering letter to the employer, it is better to send them both as PDF files.

4. Make a copy of the long document you have just created. Do not touch the original anymore. Then open the copy and cut it down. Cut it down to the essentials that correspond to the job title. Make it two pages long. Leave the minor details out – focus on important achievements. Focus on key skills.

How do you find out which details are minor? The main rule when writing a job description and person specification is that the most important responsibilities and the most needed skills are always at the top of the document. If you really have no space in your CV for the last one or two requirements mentioned in the job description and person specification, it is possible to leave them out.

However, some person specifications are constructed differently: they have essential criteria and desirable criteria for the candidates. You should definitely write how you match essential criteria in your CV, and some of the desirable ones can be left out, especially if it is hard for you think of how your experience matches them.

There is a way to fit more on your CV, though. For example, if you have three bullet points of evidence that you have great teamwork skills and only one bullet point about time management, you can create a heading *Teamwork and Organisational Skills,* where you put all four bullet points. This way, it takes less space than creating a separate heading for one bullet point, and it also looks neater.

5. After you write your CV, if you have time, leave it for a day or two. Do not think about it. Then come back to it and re-read it. Amend it if needed. If you really have no time, leave it for two hours and then edit it again.

6. Read it out loud. If it sounds bad or awkward, try to re-write it.

7. Give it to your friend to read. It's always good to have an extra pair of eyes.

8. Remember when I told you to back up your document and make a copy? All the things that you have written can be used in the future, in other CVs and other application forms for other positions. Do not delete anything – you can always use it later.

9. Take it to your university's careers service. They are professionals and can advise you even more about how to

give your CV more power. It is always good to get another opinion.

Chapter 13

Writing a Covering Letter

The covering letter is the first thing that your recruiter sees. I cannot over-emphasise its importance. It has to be impressive. It has to be professional. You must show the person who opens this letter that you care about them and their organisation. Finally, just like your CV, it should have answers to the requirements of the job description. Here are some tips how you can do it, adapted from http://www.jobsite.co.uk :

1. Presentation.

If your covering letter starts with 'Dear Sir or Madam', think again. People like to be approached personally – so take time to find out who will read your application. If the advert doesn't say it, ring the company and ask who to send the letter to. Use 'Dear Sir or Madam' only if there is no way to find out (e.g. the organisation is so large that it is not possible to know who is going to read the application – the management or the human resources, and which employee exactly).

Do not forget to put the job title at the top of the letter and reference number where applicable. If you are sending your CV and covering letter by email (most probably it will be the case), then write the job title and reference number both in the Title box and at the top of the email. You can attach your covering letter as a PDF file (send the CV as a PDF file too) and paste the covering letter into the body of the email too.

Avoid overly long paragraphs, type the letter neatly, always spell-check and never exceed one page.

Don't forget about formatting – a simple font, 12 points (11 is also applicable), one-inch margins, justified (aligned on both sides).

2. Style and Grammar

Do not start with 'I am writing in response to the job advertisement...'. It used to be very popular, but now the recruiters cannot stand this phrase anymore. Just write who you are and what your career ambitions are – this is much more useful! The job reference number at the top of the letter also informs the reader which job you are applying for.

It is better to start the letter with a sentence like 'The primary reason for my application for the position of [Job Title] at [Organisation] is...' and then state why you want this job.

Also, avoid starting each sentence with 'I' or 'my'. A part of the letter needs to focus on the company rather than yourself (see Point 5: Structure).

The language of the covering letter should be formal. Avoid contractions, colloquial expressions, slang, etc.

3. Personalise

The reader must know immediately that you have not sent this letter to another employer. General letters that seem to be 'universally applicable' impress no-one. Adjust each letter for the job you're applying for, based on the job description and person specification.

4. Content

Look at the terminology the employer has used in the job description and person specification and incorporate this into your letter. Don't forget that you need to match their needs to your experience and abilities.

5. Structure

In your opening paragraph, say who you are (student, engineer, finance expert, biologist, etc.), identify the position for which you are applying and indicate how you heard about the position. Write about yourself – your education, your qualifications, your aspirations. Explain what interests you about the job and why you would like to work in that particular field.

Next, write why the organisation interests you. Be flattering. Show that you've researched the organisation and that you care about what they're doing. Demonstrate interest, knowledge and appreciation.

Your goal in the third paragraph is to show how you can be useful to this particular organisation. Describe what strengths you have to offer by showing the relationship between your skills and experience and the vacancy. You can also describe your previous achievements and how they relate to the vacancy, and identify three reasons why you should be called to interview – again, refer to the needs of the organisation stated in the job description and person specification.

End the letter by stating what your next steps will be (See Point 10: Closing). Refer the reader to your enclosed CV for additional information.

6. Emphasise

Find relevant achievements in your work history and quote one or two succinctly and colourfully. It is fine if you have also included them in your CV – your letter should expand on your CV and complement your career summary. To some extent, your covering letter should mirror your CV, but not copy it word-for-word. Both should have some hidden elements so that they complete one another.

7. Detail

You will have researched the company as part of your preparation for the application, so when explaining why you are interested in the organisation or the position, avoid general statements like 'I am impressed with your products and growth'. Write specifically about which products, what growth and why you are impressed. Your covering letter, just like your CV, should be S.M.A.R.T. (Please see **Chapter 3: The S.M.A.R.T CV**).

8. Why you

Answer the question of 'Why you?' What makes you worth considering? What are your unique selling points? Emphasise your positive assets, such as education or skills, accomplishments and personal qualities in relation to the employer's needs. Emphasise your strengths, skills and experience.

9. Timing

If there's a closing date, time your posting so that it arrives a few days after the main 'rush' that occurs within 4-7 days of the advertisement's publication (but not after the closing date!). Alternatively, you may prefer to be the first to respond. I have applied as early as two days after the job advertisement was posted and as late as on the last day at 11.45 p.m. and got interviews. As long as it is not past the deadline, your application must be considered. However, do bear in mind that some job advertisements state that the organisation reserves the right to close the job posting if enough candidates apply and are selected for interviews before the original deadline.

10. Closing

End the letter with a specific statement of what your next step will be. If you plan to follow up with a telephone call, say so. If you plan to wait for the employer's response, say so as well. Conclude by saying you look forward to discussing your career with the advertiser.

A Sample Covering Letter

This is a sample covering letter from a student who is applying for a work placement in a science research company. It is partially based on my own covering letter which got me a placement at the Science and Technology Facilities Council. I am also going to provide an analysis of the letter.

Dear Ms Black,

Ref: COMM2018-01 Communications Officer

I am currently a Second Year student, studying English and Journalism at Anycity University, due to graduate in 2020[1]. I am writing to apply for a work placement at the Communications department at Science Research International, starting in summer 2018, with a view to a long-term career in this field[2]. The placement position in your company really interests me as it is reflects to a very large extent both my professional and personal interests.

---

[1] The student provides information about himself in the opening sentence. He talks about his academic subject (it is implied that his degree has allowed him to develop sound written communication skills, which are indispensable for a job in the field of Communications).

[2] The student tells the recruiter for which position he is applying (he also stated it at the top of the letter, mentioning the reference number) and talks about his career goals, showing that he is committed to working in a particular field.

Having undertaken research on your organisation, I am aware that your organisation is one of the leaders in the science sector, promoting and supporting pioneering research projects in the fields of electronic engineering, computer modelling, chemical engineering and green energy[3]. Moreover, it was really exciting to learn that you organise work experience for 14-16 year-old pupils. Being familiar with the present situation in the UK educational sector, I am aware that STEM subjects are not a popular area of study among prospective students, which is a great concern for the industry as scientific research motivates progress and drives the economy forward. Despite the fact that my studies are not science-related, I am enthusiastic about making change[4] and I believe that with my skills I would be able to make science more appealing to the young people.

As you can see from my CV, I have professional interest and considerable experience in representation and communications[5]. My employment history reveals my dedication and striving to maximise efficiency. I have been

---

[3] The student provides evidence that he has really undertaken research about the organisation – he knows in what areas the organisation works.

[4] The student makes a link between his career goals and a cause he believes in (education and equipping young people with practical skills).

[5] The student provides a general sentence at the start of the paragraph that introduces its contents. After that, he talks about his experience in general terms (more specific examples can be found in the CV). This is what I mean when I say that your CV and covering letter should complement each other.

actively engaged in liaising with external stakeholders of the companies that I have worked for, as well as pro-active establishment of a positive image. In addition, one of the research topics that really interests me is Global Warming and research on sustainability. I have written articles about it for *The Anycity University Herald*, and am currently organising a conference on academic research on green technologies. I possess the skills necessary for this position, being a critical researcher, having excellent command of both written and spoken English, as well as being confident, and used to working under pressure and to the deadline.

I believe that this placement would allow me to being a valuable contribution to the work of Science Research International with my education, work experience, professional skills and personal qualities. It would also provide me with an excellent opportunity of deepening and broadening my knowledge of PR, fulfilling my creative and academic potential and enhancing my professional skills required for a career in this field. I would be available for an interview at your convenience and am looking forward to hearing from you.

Yours sincerely,

Name Surname

Enclosed: CV

Chapter 14

How to Write Brilliant Application Forms

I decided to include a chapter about application forms in this book because they are an increasingly common way of recruiting people. Most of the time application forms also ask the candidate to upload a CV. Therefore, everything that I have written in this book is still relevant. However, there is another reason why the information in this book is important: application forms are basically very long CVs with very long covering letters. Sometimes you need to write more than one covering letter to support your application. I will tell you all about it, one step at a time.

Let me tell you right from the start: it is very easy to hate application forms. They are a pain in the neck, especially if you are filling one out for the first time. First of all, they are incredibly long. In the past, after I had filled out online application forms, I would often print them or save them on my computer. Guess what – while a CV and a covering letter make three pages, application forms often comprise 20-30 pages, depending on the font and on the way that online form is structured.

Application forms are long for several reasons. First of all, recruiters are busy people and they only want to review the applications made by genuinely interested candidates. What does this mean? This means that if you *really* want the job, you will bother to type all that information into the form. If you are not that keen on the job, you will not bother. It is the first way of filtering out the candidates. By the way, if you are applying for similar positions, you might have to suffer the endless process of filling in the application form only once. Later, when you apply for other jobs, you can take the information from the previous application form, copy and paste it into the new one and then modify it to fit the job description.

That is why it is a good idea to type your answers to the application form questions not directly into the online form, but into a Word document and save it for yourself later. Many online application systems allow previewing and saving your application form as well, but it is better to have the information typed somewhere where you can easily access it after you have submitted the application.

The second reason why application forms are so long is that a CV might not tell the recruiters enough about the candidate. They might need more information and a long form allows them to obtain that information.

Another challenge that you may encounter while dealing with application forms, beside their length, might be their format. The forms that you fill in online are relatively easy to manage. However, if the form is a Word document that you need to fill in and upload, there might be difficulties. Such documents can be constructed in such a way that you have very little space to write about your work experience. Some of them do not even have space for you to write about your achievements – they only have space for job titles and the dates when you held these jobs. They can also be rather restrictive about the section where you provide additional information about yourself.

In a way, application forms are a combination of three (sometimes four) things: an experience-based CV, a skills-based CV, a covering letter and (sometimes) a job interview. Let me explain what I mean.

Application forms usually contain the following sections:

1. Personal Information

This includes your name, address, telephone number, email address, etc.

2. Education.

This includes all your qualifications (university, A-levels, Secondary Education) with all your grades for all the subjects. Unlike in a CV, you might need to mention all your GCSEs. Bear in mind that many jobs require you to have passed GCSE English and Maths. Many application forms also allow you to include any training or short courses that you have undertaken. Some even have a separate section for it.

3. Work experience.

This is the place where you can truly shine. This section allows you to add all your jobs, paid and voluntary, and usually gives you a lot of space to describe your duties. However, instead of describing duties, you should describe your achievements in every position you have held. There is usually quite a lot of space to do it – some online application forms allow up to 500 words to write about each of your jobs. My advice is: if there is so much space, write as much as possible. List every single achievement you can remember from every position that you have held, making sure your text mirrors the requirements of the job description and person specification.

4. Supporting information.

This section can come in a range of forms. It can be a single field where you need to write something like a covering letter. Some application forms allow 4,000 characters, some allow between 500 and 2,000 words (the latter is quite generous as it allows you to talk in-depth about your skills). You need to provide additional information in support of your application: why you would like this job, why you would like to work for the organisation, what qualifications, skills and experience you can bring to the table, etc.

Some application forms provide a separate blank field for each of the candidate selection criteria. For example, let us take a job in which the candidate is required to have good communication skills, teamwork skills, presentation skills and experience in sales. The application form might have a separate field for each of these criteria. In this case, you should write only about communication skills (written and spoken) in the first field, giving one example (if the form says so) or as many examples as possible. The second field should be filed with examples of teamwork. The third one should be filled with experience of giving presentations, speaking in public, etc. The fourth one should contain information about your experience in sales. Some of these answers can be very long – you might need to write more than a page for each of the criteria. This is where the application form resembles a job interview: you need to answer specific questions. This is also why I said that only people who *really* want the job will be bothered to fill in the form.

5. References.

Here you need to provide contact details of two (sometimes three) people with whom you have a professional relationship. These can be your former employers and supervisors/line managers, your teachers and lecturers, etc.

These are the basic elements of most application forms. What you need to remember is that you should tailor each application form to the requirements of the job, just like with CVs.

So, this is more or less everything I would like you to know about writing CVs, covering letters and application forms.

Good luck with your job search!

SPACE FOR YOUR NOTES

Chapter 15 – Free Bonus:

Ideas and Tips on how to get some work experience while you're a student (so that you'll have something to put on your CV)

Let me begin by saying that when you are at university, you can have any job that pays the bills – because you do not need what may be called 'a serious job' to build a great CV. What you need instead is a proactive approach and willingness to dedicate your time and effort to developing new skills.

Where can you look for a simple job on campus?

Below are some ideas on where you can look for a job on campus. These are simple jobs that pay the bills:

1. The canteen

2. Campus shops – bookstore, stationery shop, food outlets

3. University pub/bar

4. Event team – flyer distribution

5. Administrative work – data entry, filling envelopes and other simple office tasks. Talk to the management offices of all departments – you might get lucky.

6. Student Representative. Some universities hire their students to tell secondary school and sixth form students how wonderful university life is and how many opportunities higher education can give. If you think you can do it, ask around – perhaps your university does this too!

The Benefits of Clubs and Societies

I can bet that in your first year you joined many clubs and societies. If you still have not, then please do so and as soon as possible! However, joining is only the first step. The next step is *doing something* for the society. As you probably know, every society has an executive committee: the president, the vice-president, the treasurer and the secretary. Each year, you are able to run for elections for one of those positions of responsibility (looks totally awesome on your CV!). However, in my view, a position is only a name, no matter how cool it sounds. What really matters is your involvement in the life of your society. This year, you need to become active and get involved as much as you can.

Here's how you can do it:

1. Help organise events.

2. Send around news and interesting items (articles, videos, podcasts etc.) that could be of interest to the members of the society.

3. Represent your society in the wider community, maybe even outside the university.

4. Take society members to events.

5. Bring interesting people relevant to the focus of the society to meet the members.

5. Become a networking geek. Be active.

6. Promote the society.

7. Increase the number of members.

8. When you succeed, put all of this down on your CV as your achievements.

And finally:

9. If you cannot find a society to which you are willing to give all your passion, then establish one!

10. Enjoy what you're doing!

The Power of Volunteering.

Volunteering has a double benefit.

First of all, **you can get a job that you normally wouldn't** at this stage – that's why it is so important to you, as a student. You can work as a PR officer, a charity fundraiser, an editor, an actor/actress, a photographer, a social worker, a journalist for a serious website… You can also work in art and design related fields. The opportunities are endless.

Secondly, your future employer will be only too pleased to see that you've invested your time and effort, learnt new skills and contributed to a greater cause. **It looks great on your CV.**

There is a lot to be gained from volunteering – skills, contacts and personal satisfaction being at the top of the list.

There are two types of volunteering: in the university and outside it. The number of opportunities depends on the size of the town/city you are living in.

Moreover, almost every university has a volunteer centre. There are numerous opportunities online too.

Check out these links:

For the United Kingdom:

http://www.volunteering.org.uk/

www.do-it.org.uk

http://www.csv.org.uk/volunteering

For the USA:

http://www.volunteermatch.org/

http://www.volunteeringinamerica.gov/

P.S. Volunteering can be a great way to get ahead for people of creative professions.

Be your own boss – become a freelancer.

If you feel you're good at something, it's worth looking into freelancing opportunities. Being a self-employed freelancer can have many benefits. You are in charge of your own schedule, have an opportunity to work from home and still gain and develop an impressive set of skills to put on your CV and make employers interested. Here are two main things you can do as a student:

1. Teaching and tutoring

Become a freelance tutor. Put up an advert on the wall in your university, advertising your skills:

- Languages (including English for foreigners)
- Maths
- IT
- Science
- Anything else you want, like graphic design or fine pottery

You can also go to a few local schools and put up your advert there.

If you are in the UK, visit these sites:

http://www.uktutors.com/

http://www.localtutor.co.uk/Tuition_Information/UK_Tutors.html

http://www.firsttutors.com/uk/

You can register on those sites as a freelance tutor in any field from art design to zoology, and set your rates. I advise you to be prudent and not charge too much – after all, you are only a student, not a professional with a PhD and 10 years of experience.

2. Translation and Interpreting

Speak another language? Try freelance translation and interpreting. Just find out email addresses of all the translation agencies around you and apply to all of them. Even as a student, you can get plenty of work and use your language skills. It is also a really rewarding job when you realise you're helping people communicate!

Other books by Vlad Mackevic

From Confusion to Conclusion: How to Write
a First-Class Essay (2nd Edition)

Fight for that Job! How to become
employable while you are still at university

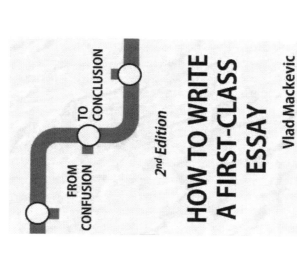

How to Write First-Class Business Essays and Dissertations: Advice to Business, Economics, Finance, Marketing and Management Students from a First-Class Graduate

How to Write First-Class Business Essays and Dissertations

Vlad Mackevic

Amazon Kindle #1 Bestselling Author
College and University Section

SPACE FOR YOUR NOTES

SPACE FOR YOUR NOTES